# BOOK ANALYSIS

Written by Hadrien Seret
Translated by Emma Lunt

AF126350

# Journey to the End of the Night

BY LOUIS-FERDINAND CÉLINE

# LOUIS-FERDINAND CÉLINE

## FRENCH DOCTOR AND WRITER

- **Born in Courbevoie (France) in 1894**
- **Died in Meudon in 1961**
- **Notable works:**
  - *Death on Credit* (1936), novel
  - *Cannon-Fodder* (1949), novel
  - *North* (1960), novel

Louis Ferdinand Destouches, known as Céline, was a French author who was born in 1894 and died in 1961. He is considered one of the major novelists of the 20<sup>th</sup> century for his works, including *Journey to the End of the Night* (1932) and *Death on Credit* (1936).

A trained doctor, he drew the main inspiration for his literary works from an unusual life path which saw him visit multiple destinations (England, Cameroon, USA) and try different jobs. The experiences that resulted from this served as the foundation for the condemnation of the hardships of his era. This process led him to form opinions that were difficult to reconcile (from free healthcare for the poor to his notorious antisemitism) which would make him one of the most contested writers of French literature.

# *JOURNEY TO THE END OF THE NIGHT*

## THE UPS AND DOWNS OF A CONDEMNATION

- **Genre:** novel
- **Reference edition:** Céline, L-F. (1983) *Journey to the End of the Night*. Trans. Manheim, R. New York: New Directions Publishing Corporation.
- **First edition:** 1932
- **Themes:** happiness, search, journey, colonies, poverty, the First World War

Published in 1932 and awarded the Prix Renaudot (French literary prize) that same year, *Journey to the End of the Night* is the novel that brought Céline his fame and granted him his place as a legitimate player in literature.

In this book, filled with his characteristic prose, the writer castigates the refusal of the world (and particularly of Europe in the Roaring Twenties) to see its own poverty in favour of running towards fanciful pleasures that only aggravate the situation rather than improving it.

The author therefore portrays, through the experience of his narrator, Bardamu, an unforgiving image of this era that immediately followed the First World War. It is an original and dissonant portrait which is universally impacted by the hero's different journeys.

# SUMMARY

In order to provide the clearest summary possible, we have chosen not to follow the divisions used in the book and have instead opted to separate the sections by journey. The story's chronology has been maintained.

## PARIS AND THE FIRST WORLD WAR

Paris. In search of recognition and out of bravado towards a friend that is with him, Ferdinand Bardamu decides to follow a troop and join the army. However, the everyday life of a world war is not as heroic as he had expected: he discovers the horror and indignity of a battle of which he understands neither the aim nor the functioning. One day, during a reconnaissance mission, he comes face to face with Robinson, an army reserve whose ambition is to abandon the army. Shortly after their encounter, Bardamu is gravely injured and repatriated to the French capital.

Celebrated as a war hero, Ferdinand revels for a short moment in his notoriety and tries to forget the horrors that he has lived through. But very quickly, he realises the hypocrisy of the situation: the false value of the medals, the enthusiasm of women and nurses to sleep with him just to grab their claim to fame (for example, Musyne) or even the haste with which injured soldiers create ploys in order to not return to combat. Paris itself is the image of prevailing hypocrisy: the city is in the midst of economic decline even though everything seems to be going well. Nauseated by this atmosphere and by his status as a soldier, Bardamu finally recovers after two more trips to hospital. Later, another encounter with Robinson pushes the hero to leave for an adventure in Africa, in the colonies.

## THE COLONIES (FORT-GONO, TOPO)

After a stormy journey by sea where he is almost lynched by the crew and passengers, Bardamu finally disembarks at Fort-Gono. There, he discovers that life is lot more difficult than he had imagined; he cannot acclimatise to the precarious comfort, the stifling heat, the illnesses nor the many insatiable insects. The natives, for their part, intrigue him greatly and he divides his time between observing them and insulting them.

Motivated by his desire to succeed, the protagonist manages to find work at a stall in Topo. The journey there is difficult, and Bardamu is weak when he reaches his new destination and meets the man he must replace, who turns out to be none other than Robinson. The latter runs away in the cover of night toward new horizons, ensuring to bring the kiosk with him.

Together with two colleagues (Alcide and Grappa), Bardamu leads a poor existence, punctuated by sudden high fevers. The day his hut begins to burn, he realises that the colonies will not bring him the wealth he desires: he therefore leaves Africa for the United States.

## THE UNITED STATES (NEW YORK, DENVER)

Despite his ship being quarantined, Bardamu manages

to get into the city of New York. There, he is fascinated to discover the skyscrapers, Manhattan, Broadway, the banks, the shops, the shining cinema, the immense hotels and mazes (the *Laugh Calvin*) and, above all, the dollar, which he likens to a god. Day after day, the narrator sees his limited colonial savings dissolve like snow in the sun. While at first he manages to extort money from his former mistress (Lola), he must quickly resign himself to finding another way to earn his keep. Thus, he leaves for Detroit to get a job at Ford. In this fast-growing company, he finds himself faced with the realities of factory line work, infuriating working schedules and low pay. Luckily, his meeting with and then attachment to the prostitute, Molly, gives him the strength to carry on.

One night, he meets Robinson on a tram. Robinson convinces the narrator to return to France, where he will join him once his situation has been resolved. Against Molly's advice, he takes to the sea once again, this time in the direction of his homeland.

## LA GARENNE-CLICHY

Many years pass. Having returned to his studies and earned his medicine degree, Bardamu establishes himself as a practitioner in La Garenne-Clichy. As this town already has many doctors, life is difficult for the hero who is often called as a last resort by clients who do not pay him. This free service makes him seem like a bad doctor. Haunted by the fear of not being able to heal others, he sees before him a parade of the woes of the world: a failed abortion, a labour gone wrong, the Henrouille couple who try to corrupt him in order to send their mother-in-law to the asylum or even his friend Bébert who he cannot save from typhoid. To top it all off, Robinson, who has returned to France, harasses him endlessly about these anxieties. Robinson must even receive emergency care from his old friend, after an elaborate plan that he masterminded with the aim of killing the Henrouilles' mother-in-law turns against him and he injures his eyes. With the timely help of the priest, Protiste, Bardamu sends Robinson to Toulouse to recover. During this time, he himself volunteers at a small clinic before being granted the role of a pasha in a little Parisian cabaret, which allows him to discover show business, its joys and its tragedies.

He is then invited to Toulouse by Robinson who is gradually regaining his sight and about to marry Madelon. As for the Henrouilles' mother-in-law, she is doing well and pays a visit to a lucrative vault filled with mummified tourists.

On returning to Paris, Bardamu finds employment at an asylum run by Baryton, a psychiatrist. After the narrator has taught him English, Baryton gives Ferdinand the keys to his establishment and leaves for Great Britain. Somehow handling his new job with the help of his friend Paraphine, Robinson one day turns up at the hero's institution, looking for a place to hide from Madelon who he no longer tolerates and does not want to marry. The doctor is diplomatic and tries to reconcile the couple, but this attempt becomes tragic: in the face of Robinson's categorical refusal to marry her, Madelon shoots him and he dies a few hours later in

Bardamu's arms.

# CHARACTER STUDY

## FERDINAND BARDAMU

Ferdinand Bardamu is the narrator and the main protagonist in *Journey to the End of the Night*. He is a recurring figure in Céline's works, as he can also be found in other books in which he plays a hero or a secondary character (notably in *Death on Credit* and *The Church*).

Throughout the work, Bardamu evolves. It is possible to distinguish two steps in his development. The first covers the three opening sections and can be considered as the training of his era. We can see that for each of the three sections, the author uses the same narrative pattern, which is:

- A phase of wonderment where Bardamu builds his hopes for a better life (the heroic image of the army, the adventurous side of the colonies, the innovative aspect of pioneering American modernity).
- A return to reality phase: Bardamu's aspirations are halted by obstacles (often financial) which provide him with a harsh reality check (his injury on the battle field, the fevers and poverty in Africa, the tiresome work at Ford in the United States).
- A criticism phrase: by confronting the reality of things (often through work), Bardamu becomes aware that all the appearances of a better life that he sees around him are only illusions. Furthermore, they only benefit some people.

This triple journey, which we could see as a rite of passage, highlights one of the main characteristics of this character; the impossibility of happiness. As happiness has an illusory character in the world in which he lives, the hero cannot record his joy in a lasting way. We see this very clearly in his love life (see the situation with Musyne, Lola or Molly) or in friendship (in the intermittent relationship he shares with Robinson or his friendship with Paraphine which ends in silence).

The second of Bardamu's development stages takes place in the fourth section, in Rancy. By choosing to become a doctor, the hero gives his existence some consistency, an anchorage point which puts an end to the ups and downs of the first three parts. As if to accentuate this change within his character, Céline puts in an interval of several years so that the reader immediately finds themselves faced with a much more mature Bardamu. He is no longer an actor in a story but an observer of the suffering of which he has become aware (for example, the very detailed descriptions of the torments of the sick that come to visit him) and that he tries to relieve in his own way.

## LÉON ROBINSON

Léon Robinson is a character of special status in *Journey to the End of the Night*. A mysterious man, Robinson is somebody who is constantly searching for this illusory happiness to which he introduces Bardamu and which the latter ends up rejecting. In the first part of the story, he takes on the role of the guide, who opens the door for the hero's own experiences, to the point where Bardamu considers him as a role model to follow in order to achieve success. He is therefore stunned by his bad luck in the United States: "What I hadn't expected was that he too was a failure in America. That came as a surprise" (p. 200).

Robinson does not achieve anything despite his perseverance. However, his desire to live happily (and be rich) is so strong that it pushes him to accept all sorts of tasks, even the most sordid ones: for example, we see him prepare a trap to kill the Henrouilles' mother-in-law in the hope of earning a large sum of money. However, like Bardamu, Robinson is struck by the impossibility of achieving happiness no matter what he does (which can be seen in his love story with Madelon). But despite his numerous failings, he refuses to change and clings onto a goal that he will never achieve, which Bardamu reproaches him for strongly: "'You're a bourgeois!' I told him finally [...]. 'All you ever think of is money... Once you recover your eyesight, you'll be the worst of the whole bunch'" (p. 339). Thus, the self-sacrifice and selflessness that the doctor shows in the fourth section opposes the adventurer's appetite for wealth and his wish to enjoy temporary pleasures. This antagonism triggers the progressive breakdown of their friendship as well as a role reversal in their relationship: we see Robinson become dependent on Bardamu, contrary to before (we see this when Bardamu agrees to hide his friend in his asylum).

However, Robinson ends up freeing himself from this illusion of happiness by refusing the final advances of Madelon. But for a character that is fully focused on this illusion, this act can only end in death.

.

# ANALYSIS

## *JOURNEY TO THE END OF THE NIGHT*: EXPLANATION OF THE TITLE

While, at the end of the novel, the choice to incorporate the word 'journey' into the title is clearly justified, the association of 'night' and especially 'end', which are never really made explicit, can be surprising or even throw the reader off balance. It is not that darkness is absent from the plot: on the contrary, it is omnipresent, whether simply as a spatiotemporal indicator or in metaphors, sometimes positive, sometimes negative (night as a moment of relaxation or dreaming; night as a conveyor of loneliness or anxiety, etc.). However, through one particular phrase, Céline points towards a better understanding: "That's what life is, a bit of light that ends the darkness" (p. 294). The nocturnal atmosphere symbolises an atmosphere where neither life nor any material and psychological desires can survive. Thus, Bardamu and Robinson's travels to obtain happiness resemble an impossible mission as they are trying to have something that does not exist.

In the same general idea, refusing – as the two protagonists do – this logic about the illusion that rules the world, is refusing to live. Consequently, the "end of the night" is, simply, dying: Robinson dives headfirst into this ending while Bardamu just remains on the border, clear-headed about the laws that rule his existence but without totally refusing them (which is seen in his adventure with Sophie), allowing him to tell the reader the story of his life.

# THE CONTEXT OF THE TEXT AND THE CONDEMNATION: THE START OF THE 20<sup>TH</sup> CENTURY

*Journey to the End of the Night* is not only a story about a rite of passage and its consequences. It is also a vibrant indictment of the early 20<sup>th</sup> century, a time portrayed as being in the midst of breakdown and basking in a type of artificial joy, allowing people not to notice all of the destitution around them.

This condemnation appears in the work's four sections; each reflects a very specific reality.

### Part one: The First World War

Céline highlights two ideas in his description of the conflict:

- The first is the carnage that such a conflict causes and the lack of understanding regarding the reasons that led to the fighting ("As far back as I could search my memory, I hadn't done a thing to the Germans", p. 7).
- The second is the willingness of the Parisian population to forget that it is at war and to live as if nothing is happening. Céline criticises particularly strongly the nurses' thirst for fame, the cowardice of the injured soldiers, the splendour of notoriety and those that profit from the war (such as Madame Hérote).

Céline therefore deplores in his text the artificial side of life: there is no true love or true heroism, just an atmosphere of suffering that everybody ignores by turning towards false gratification.

## Part two: The colonies

In this section, the writer tries to break the stereotypes of colonies as some sort of exotic 'El Dorado'. He portrays the French companies as being greedy for riches and not hesitating to exploit the indigenous people in the harshest ways. He also describes the so-called courageous adventurers who are nothing more than foreigners suffering from the climate and victims of the hope of a quick fortune that turns out to be unreal. This description is also the chance for the author to question whether the natives or the non-natives are the most likely to be savages.

## Part three: The American dream

The years that follow the First World War turn out to be prosperous for the United States. The country is in full economic prosperity and sees its technology, as well as its cities, progressing rapidly: the symbol of excellence of this double dynamic is unarguably Detroit, that develops under the authority of the renowned Ford factories. But such companies need a colossal workforce. This comes from the depopulation of rural America but also from the many people that leave a ruined Europe in the hope of a better life. However, most of the time, it is only a mind-numbing and badly paid job awaits them. Worked to the bone by their employers, they are nothing more than a dehumanised and automated mass that works for the comfort of a few. It is this dehumanisation that Céline castigates; an opposing opinion at a time when everybody was fascinated by America.

**Part four: The poverty of the working class (Rancy)**

Here, Céline paints a portrait of an urban working class that is suffering the worst sorrows in complete anonymity. He also highlights the inconsideration that the main protagonist suffers despite the relief that he tries to provide for this social class. This last section of *Journey to the End of the Night* is why the novel is often said to be targeted at the working-class.

## A PLOT WRITTEN WITH A UNIQUE STYLE

One of Louis-Ferdinand Céline's trademarks is unarguably his writing style: he uses a written transcription of popular, spoken language. While this process is far from original in itself (it had already been used by authors such as Eugène Dabit), the author nevertheless distinguishes himself by using it throughout his book and not only in dialogue. This choice is not insignificant: it demonstrates the writer's desire to reproduce, in writing, the emotion of everyday conversation. By adopting such a position, he deliberately puts himself in a delicate position with classic authors, whose writing style he deems too abstruse and cold.

The following sentence is a good example of this particular style:

> "I'd never been able to stomach the country, I'd always found it dreary, those endless fields, those houses where nobody's ever home, those roads that don't go anywhere" (p. 8).

Indeed, within this quotation we find many popular traits

such as useless repetitions (for example, the repetition of 'those') and the use of contractions ('I'd, 'nobody's', 'don't'). Nevertheless, this stylistic choice does not stop a certain meticulousness in the writing: for example, in this extract, we can see an anaphora ('I'd [...], I'd').

# FURTHER REFLECTION

## SOME QUESTIONS TO THINK ABOUT...

- In *Journey to the End of the Night*, is Robinson's character a guide, a sign or an anti-hero? Explain your answer.
- What arguments could convince the reader that Bardamu is a fictional character? And what arguments could be used to prove that he is the author's alter ego?
- Why is Céline interested in writing about an event such as the First World War?
- Explain how each of the places that Bardamu visits offers the chance for Céline to condemn a particular thing.
- In what way can we say that the novel opens and closes in silence? How does this analysis bring another dimension to Bardamu's story?
- Bearing in mind the era in which the novel was written, can we consider Bardamu's remarks about the black people in Africa as racism?
- How do we know that Céline's job as a doctor plays a vital role in the plot itself and its development?
- How is the contrast between American modernity and the dehumanisation of workers at Ford representative of Céline's concept of the illusion of happiness?
- How can the appearance of Bardamu's selflessness and the confirmation of Robinson's financial greed be compared to a shared journey dividing in two?

*We want to hear from you!*
*Leave a comment on your online library*
*and share your favourite books on social media!*

# FURTHER READING

## REFERENCE EDITION

- Céline, L-F. (1983) *Journey to the End of the Night*. Trans. Manheim, R. New York: New Directions Publishing Corporation.

## REFERENCE STUDIES

- Alméras, P. (2004) *Dictionnaire Céline*. Paris: Plon.
- De Phalèse, H. (1993) *Guide de Voyage au bout de la nuit: Voyage au bout de la nuit à travers les nouvelles technologies*. Paris: Nizet.
- Latin, D. (1988) *Le Voyage au bout de la nuit de Céline: roman de la subversion et subversion du roman: langue, fiction, écriture*. Brussels: Palais des Académies.
- Morand-Devillier, J. (2010) *Les idées politiques de Louis-Ferdinand Céline*. Paris: Écriture.
- Vitoux, F. (1978) *Céline*. Paris: Pierre Belfond.

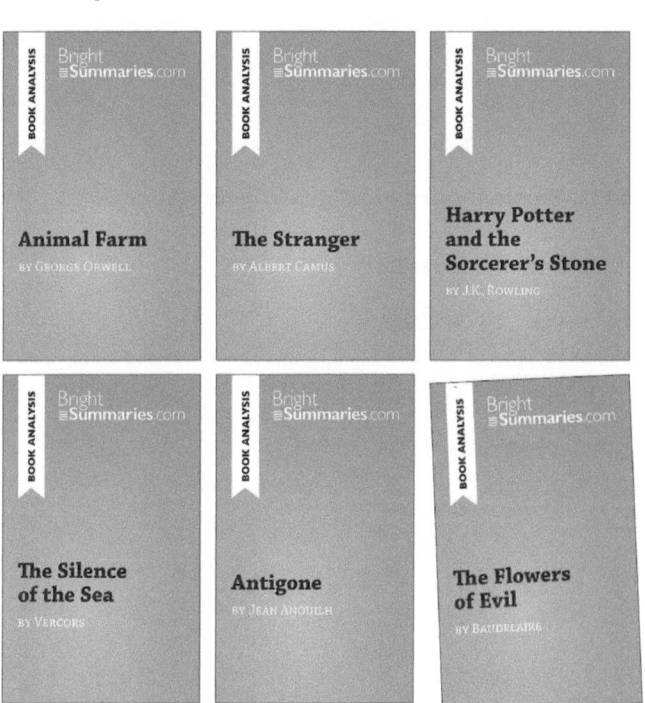